AF425400

INITIAL CONSONANT BLENDS
FOR 1ST GRADE VOLUME 1

Reading Book for Kids

Children's Reading and Writing Books

Speedy Publishing LLC

40 E. Main St. #1156

Newark, DE 19711

www.speedypublishing.com

Copyright 2017

All Rights reserved. No part of this book may be reproduced or used in any way or form or by any means whether electronic or mechanical, this means that you cannot record or photocopy any material ideas or tips that are provided in this book.

Everything in this world is filled with words. Let's discover these words through learning Consonat blends.

CONSONANT BLENDS

Consonant Blends are group of two or three consonants in a word that produce a consonant sound.

LIST OF CONSONANT DIGRAPHS

bl	br	ch	cl	cr	dr	fl
sh	sk	sl	sm	sn	sp	st
sch	scr	shr	sph	spl	spr	squ
gl	gr	pl	pr	th	tr	wh
thr	tw	wr	sc	str	sw	fr

Let's discover words that have Consonant blends with these activities!

Name: _______________________

Form words with the consonant blend **bl**.
Add the end of the word to **bl** and write it below.
Say the word. For example: **bl** + **imp** = **blimp**

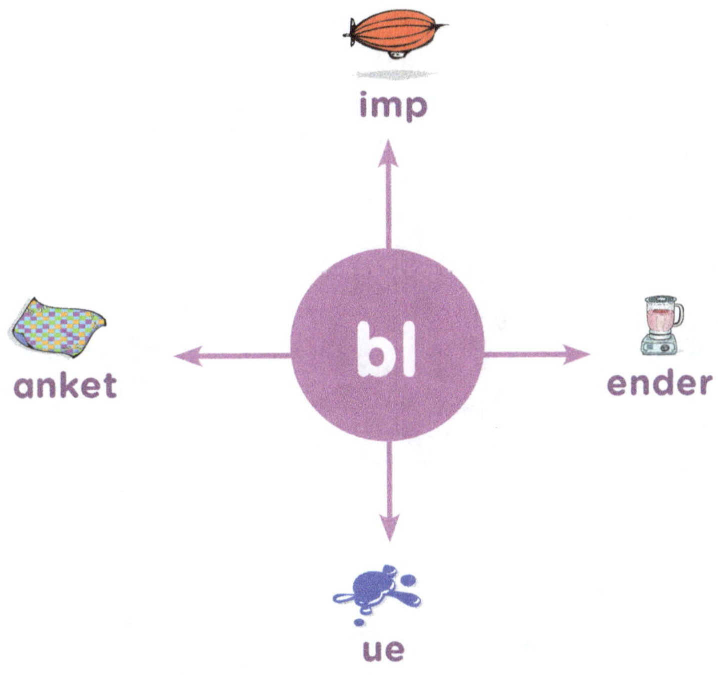

1 **BLIMP**

2 _______________

3 _______________

4 _______________

Name: _______________________

Form words with the consonant blend **br**.
Add the end of the word to **br** and write it below.
Say the word. For example: **br** + **ead** = **bread**

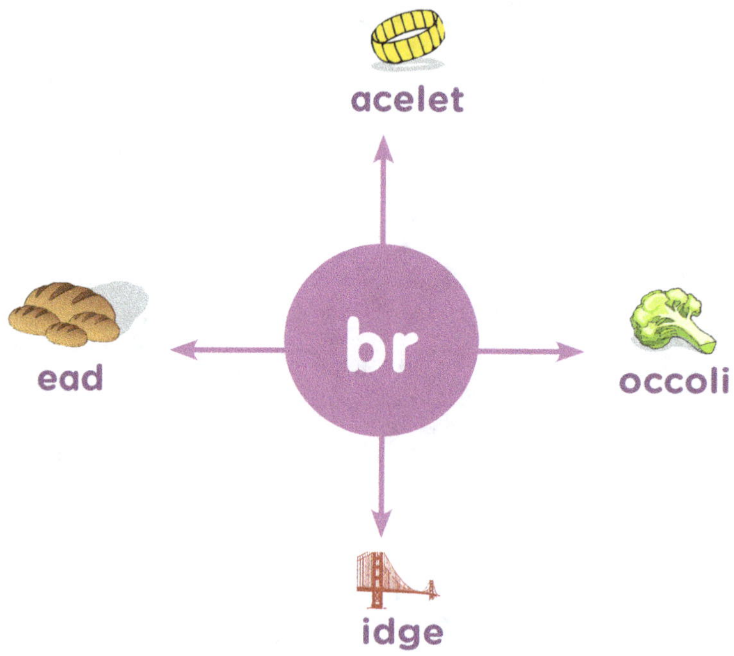

1 **BREAD**

2 _______________________

3 _______________________

4 _______________________

Name: ___________________

 Form words with the consonant blend **cl**.
Add the end of the word to **cl** and write it below.
Say the word. For example: **cl** + **ock** = **clock**

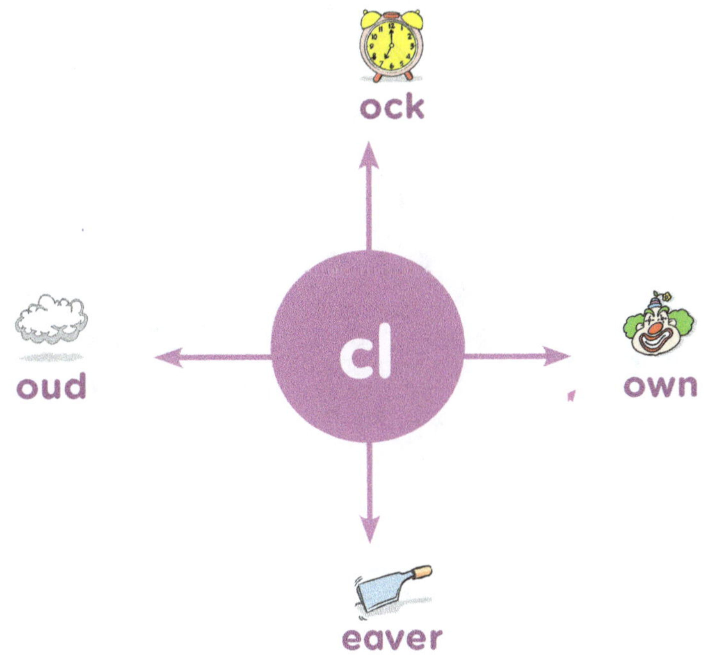

1 **CLOCK**

2 _______________

3 _______________

4 _______________

Form words with the consonant blend **cr**.
Add the end of the word to **cr** and write it below.
Say the word. For example: **cr** +**ayon** = **crayon**

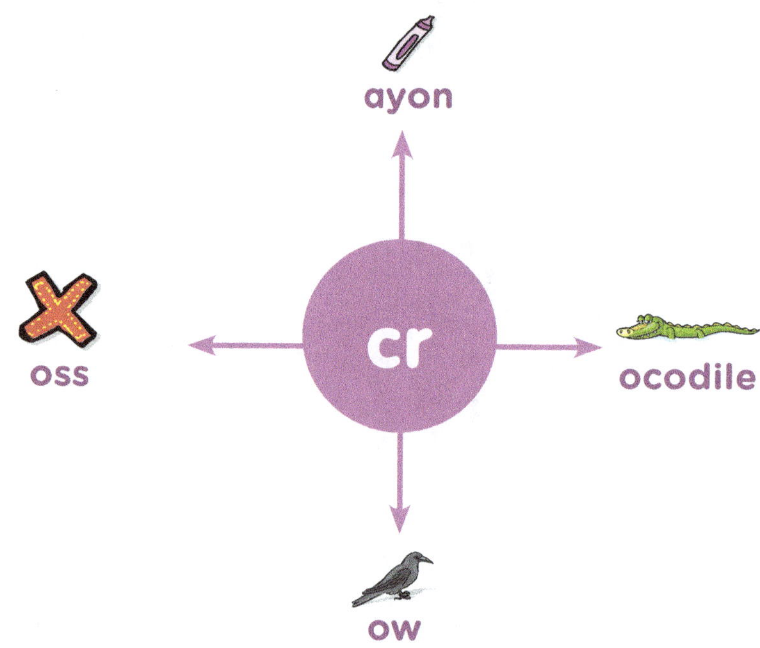

1 CRAYON

2 ______________________

3 ______________________

4 ______________________

Form words with the consonant blend **dr**.
Add the end of the word to **dr** and write it below.
Say the word. For example: **dr** + **ink** = **drink**

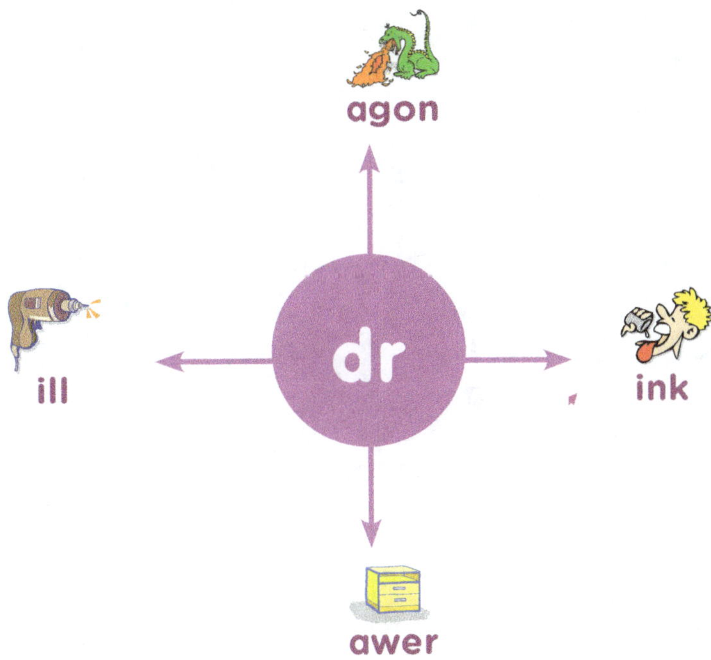

1 **DRINK**

3 _______________

2 _______________

4 _______________

Form words with the consonant blend **st**.
Add the end of the word to **st** and write it below.
Say the word. For example: **st** + **amp** = **stamp**

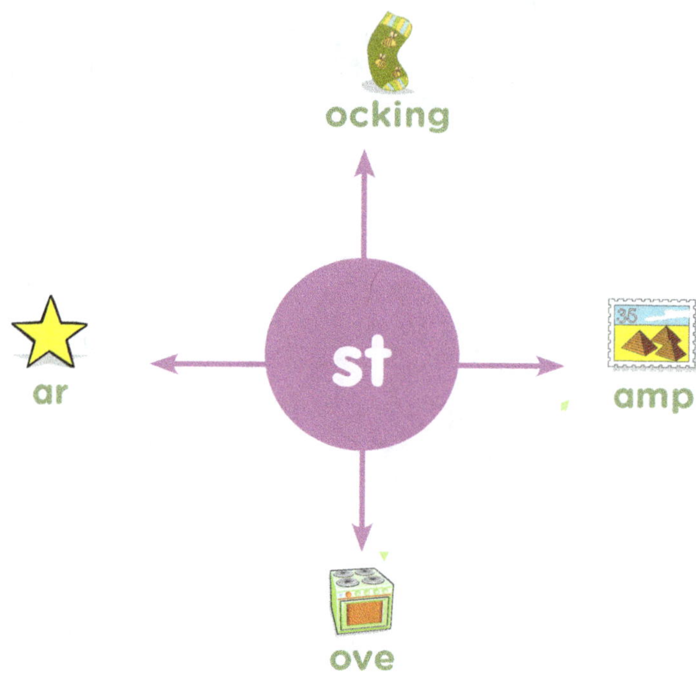

1 **STAMP**

3 _______________________

2 _______________________

4 _______________________

Name: ___________________________

Form words with the consonant blend **fl** .
Add the end of the word to **fl** and write it below.
Say the word. For example: **fl** + **ower** = **flower**

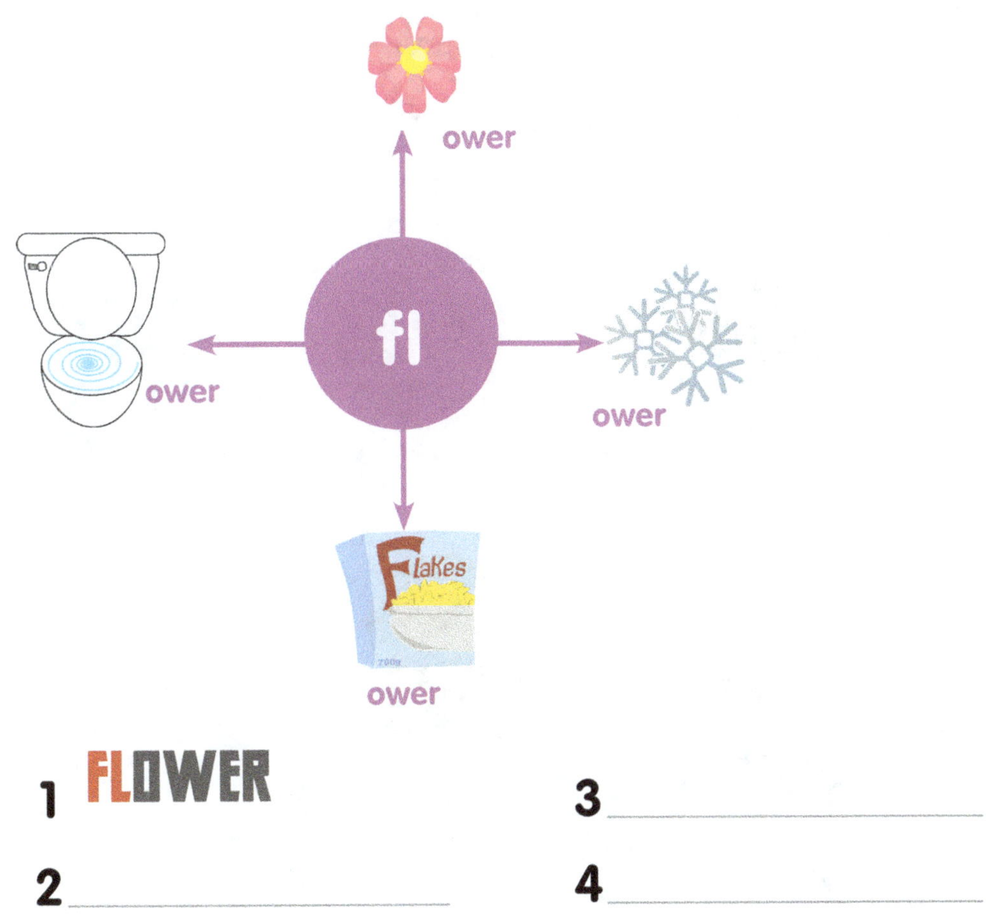

1 **FLOWER**

2 _______________________

3 _______________________

4 _______________________

Name: ________________________

Form words with the consonant blend **sl** .
Add the end of the word to **sl** and write it below.
Say the word. For example: **sl** + **lice** = **sllice**

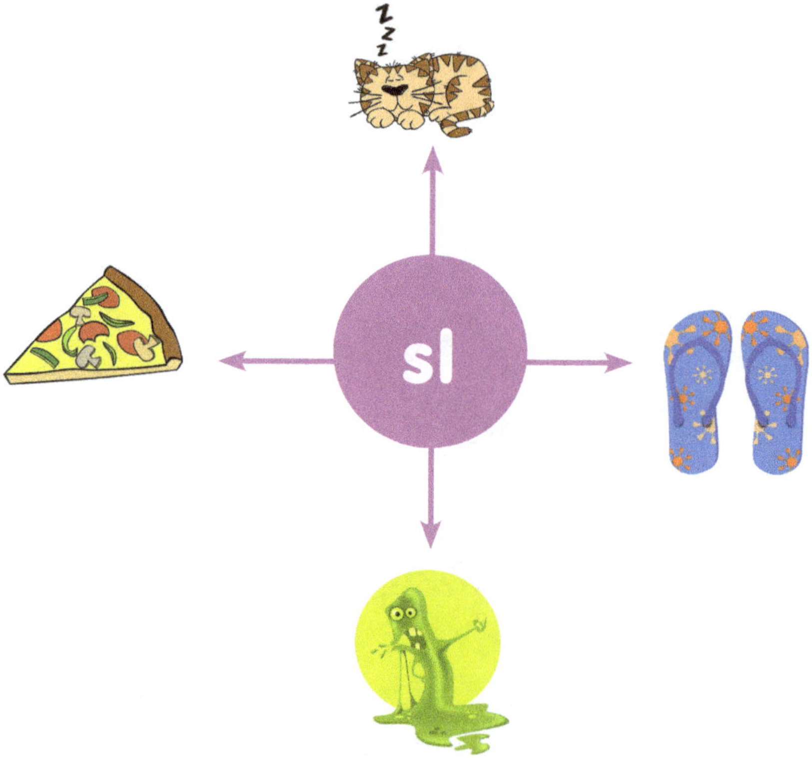

1 **SL LICE**

2 ___________________

3 ___________________

4 ___________________

Name: _______________________

Form words with the consonant blend **sh**.
Add the end of the word to **sh** and write it below.
Say the word. For example: **sh** + **ip** = **ship**

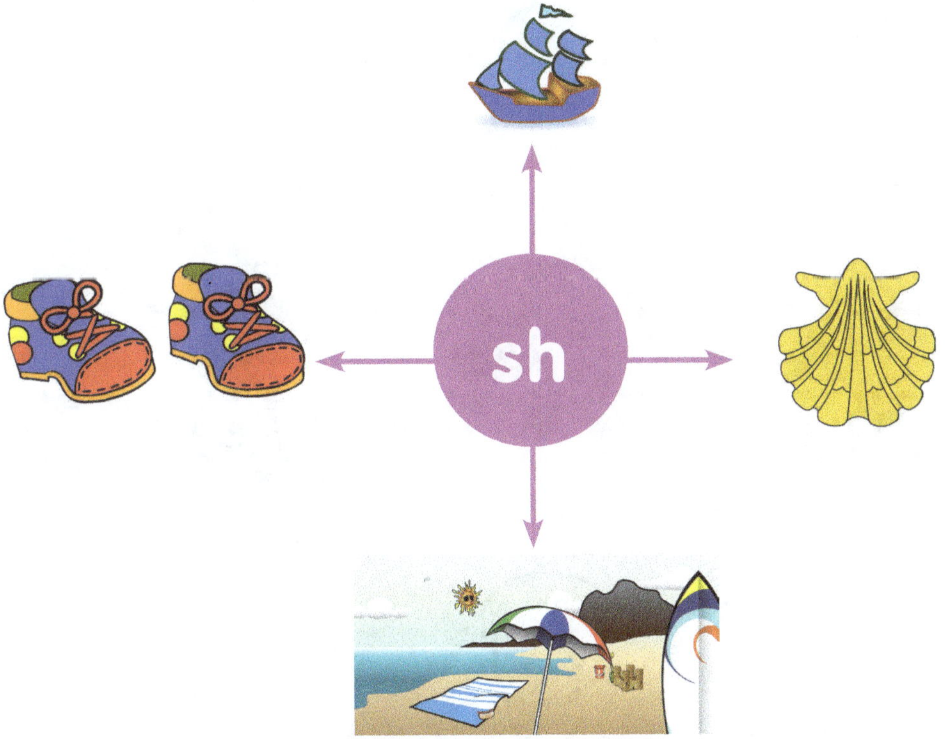

sh

1 **SHIP**

2 _______________

3 _______________

4 _______________

Form words with the consonant blend **sk**.
Add the end of the word to **sk** and write it below.
Say the word. For example: **sk** + **y** = **sky**

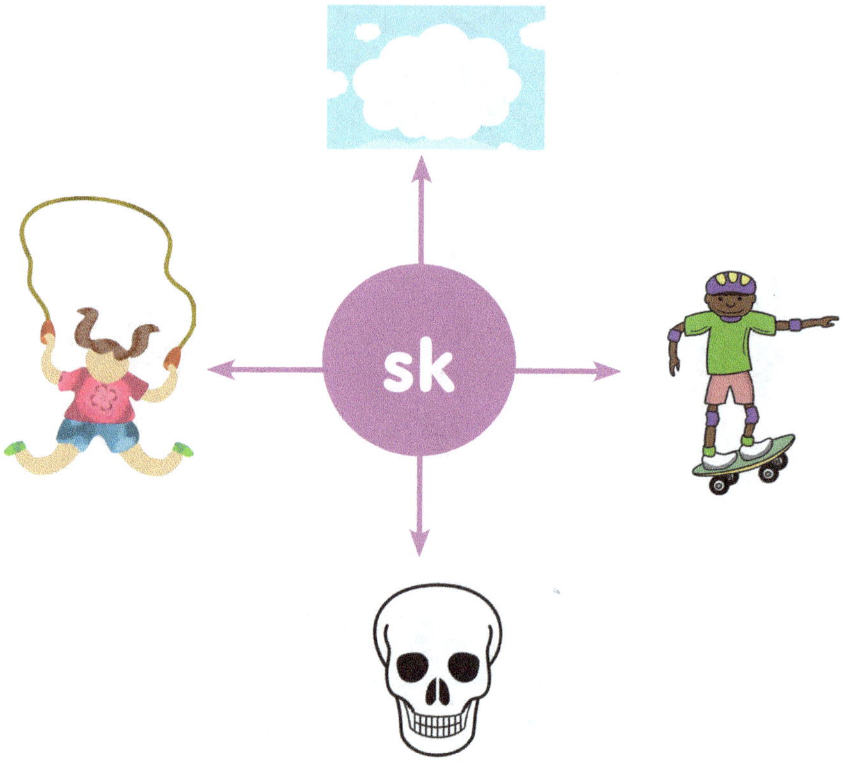

1 **SKY**

2 _______________

3 _______________

4 _______________

Form words with the consonant blend **sm**.
Add the end of the word to **sm** and write it below.
Say the word. For example: **sm** + **all** = **small**

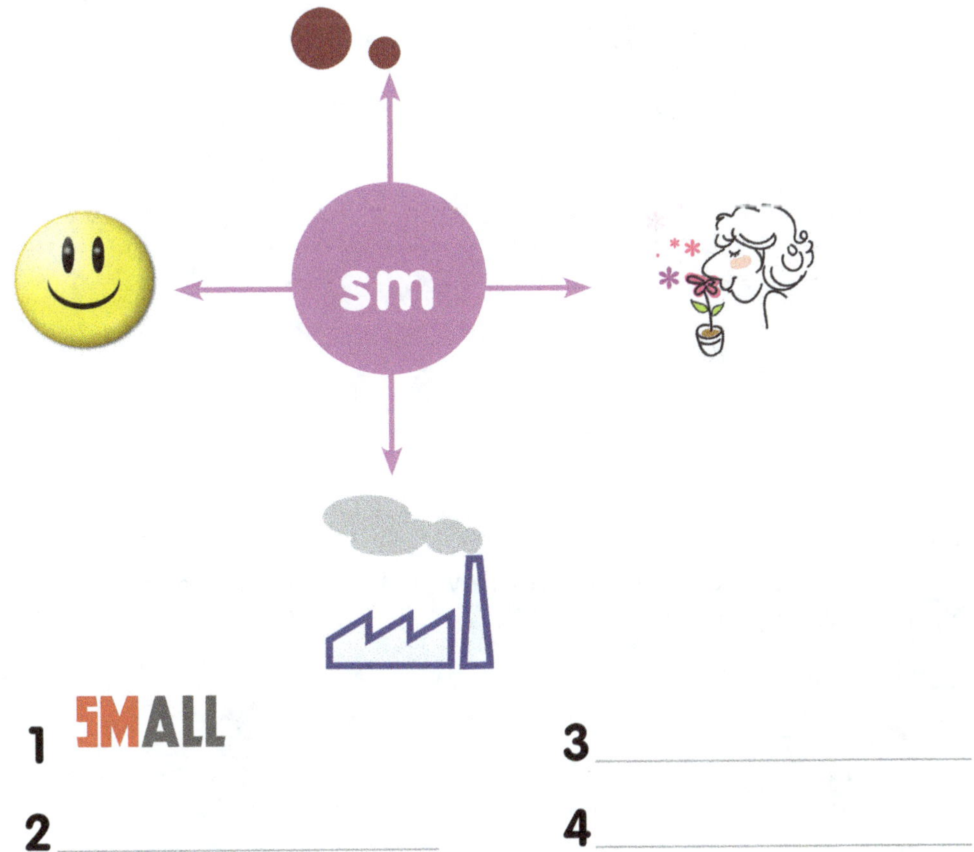

1 **SMALL**

2 _______________

3 _______________

4 _______________

First, say the word. Add the correct missing letters to complete the word. Compare the sounds of the words with **br** against those with **pr**.

br

_______ide

_______ay

pr

_______ide

_______ay

Read the sentences below and underline words with **br** or **pr**.

First, say the word. Add the correct missing letters to complete the word. Compare the sounds of the words with **cr** against those with **gr**.

cr   gr

______   ______

____oss   ____oss

______   ______

____ew   ____ew

Read the sentences below and underline words with **cr** or **gr**.

First, say the word. Add the correct missing letters to complete the word. Compare the sounds of the words with **dr** against those with **tr**.

dr   tr

_____ain   _____ain

_____ip   _____ip

_____unk   _____unk

Read the sentences below and underline words with **dr** or **tr**.

First, say the word. Add the correct missing letters to complete the word. Compare the sounds of the words with **fr** against those with **fl**.

fr

____

____y

____

____og

fl

____

____y

____

____og

Read the sentences below and underline words with **fr** or **fl**.

Name: _______________________

 Say the word. Write the correct beginning to complete the word.

 ____ air

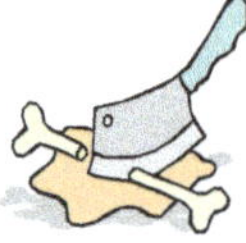 ____ op

 ____ ick

 ____ ain

 Say the sentence. Underline words that start with **ch**.

Say the word. Write the correct beginning to complete the word.

sh ip

_____ op

_____ oe

_____ eep

Say the sentence. Underline words that start with **sh**.

Name: ________________________

Say the word. Write **th** at the beginning of each word, to complete the words with the voiceless /**th**/ sound.

3 ___ree   ___umb

___ink   ___row

Say the sentence below. Underline words that start with **th**.

The letters **wh** make the sound /**hw**/ as in **whale**.
Say the word. Write the correct beginning to complete the word.

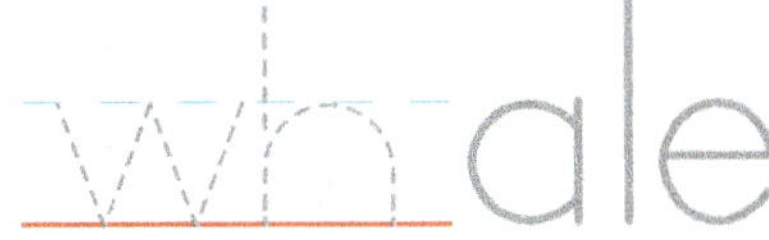

Trace the first words of the questions.
Read the questions.

What   is your name?

When   is your birthday?

Why   are you late?

The digraph **ph** makes the sound /**f**/ as in **ph**oto.
Trace the letters and say the word.

phone  photo

pheasant

photographer

elephant

Read the sentences below. Circle words with **ph** or **f**.
Say the words again.

First, the photographer photographed the pheasant. Then he photographed the elephant. Finally, he phoned my father to pick up the photos.

First, say the word. Add the correct missing letters to complete the word. Compare the sounds of the words with **spl** against those with **spr**.

spl

_____ int

_____ ay

spr

_____ int

_____ ay

Read the sentences below and underline words with **spl** or **spr**.

B	M	B	R	U	T	A	L	I	S
R	G	H	Z	X	W	U	U	C	Y
U	V	L	J	T	O	I	X	Z	V
N	E	Q	B	B	B	B	E	I	C
E	F	P	Q	X	R	R	U	N	Z
T	E	D	X	M	I	U	U	U	H
T	Z	Q	K	J	R	T	I	S	Q
E	B	R	O	W	S	E	W	S	H
Y	I	L	G	G	I	S	Q	E	E
C	Q	V	R	F	D	F	D	H	M

Circle the words that contains the consonant blend below:

br

There are 5 possible words in the puzzle! Have fun!

Write the Words!

Write the words found in the puzzle on the lines below:

Name: ______________________

U	F	O	I	S	C	O	S	S	W
W	I	C	K	I	H	I	E	S	Y
J	Z	H	M	L	U	T	H	A	R
P	L	O	C	R	R	S	Q	H	C
I	F	O	H	P	C	Q	N	G	H
X	F	S	O	H	H	P	F	G	O
M	O	E	P	C	H	O	R	E	S
N	G	V	Q	D	K	Q	O	B	E
P	A	X	N	R	D	D	A	A	F
P	A	E	T	R	R	M	A	D	S

Circle the words that contains the consonant blend below:

ch

There are 5 possible words in the puzzle! Have fun!

Write the Words!

Write the words found in the puzzle on the lines below:

Name: ______________________

Circle the words that contains the consonant blend below:

cl

Y	B	Q	M	C	L	U	M	S	Y
X	J	C	E	A	N	G	G	Z	D
F	A	L	C	C	A	Q	X	L	Y
V	X	U	L	L	E	C	M	D	F
Z	Q	N	U	U	Z	L	P	G	J
A	K	K	T	S	C	U	Q	R	X
C	A	Y	T	T	K	T	P	U	B
M	A	Q	E	E	R	C	N	V	T
M	C	K	R	R	K	H	B	W	D
J	S	K	N	B	Y	A	X	Z	T

There are 5 possible words in the puzzle! Have fun!

Write the Words!

Write the words found in the puzzle on the lines below:

Name: _______________________

Circle the words that contains the consonant blend below:

dr

V	D	O	G	Q	J	M	G	G	S
P	Q	R	D	R	U	G	W	T	V
R	T	R	U	A	J	T	M	K	J
M	O	Q	R	N	Y	N	E	A	F
S	E	U	Q	O	K	C	O	D	K
L	L	Y	X	F	W	L	H	R	H
C	E	Z	D	D	P	F	L	U	E
T	D	B	S	R	V	I	S	M	N
P	R	K	E	P	Y	A	A	F	O
M	Y	Y	H	A	M	M	H	S	F

There are 5 possible words in the puzzle! Have fun!

Write the Words!

Write the words found in the puzzle on the lines below:

U	F	O	I	S	F	O	S	S	W
W	I	F	K	I	L	I	E	S	Y
J	Z	L	M	L	O	T	H	A	R
P	L	I	F	R	G	S	Q	H	F
I	F	T	L	P	Q	N	G	X	L
F	H	P	O	F	G	M	O	N	O
G	V	Q	A	F	L	O	C	K	E
D	K	Q	T	O	B	P	A	X	N
R	D	D	A	A	F	P	A	E	T
R	R	M	A	D	S	W	F	N	V

Circle the words that contains the consonant blend below:

fl

There are 5 possible words in the puzzle! Have fun!

Write the Words!

Write the words found in the puzzle on the lines below:

Name: _______________________

Circle the words that contains the consonant blend below:

Q	R	K	G	L	U	M	T	R	B
M	K	P	Q	J	L	W	Y	C	N
L	J	V	M	F	V	J	G	U	A
D	F	J	U	M	P	G	L	U	E
R	N	T	C	G	Y	G	U	I	K
N	D	S	P	L	Q	L	T	V	E
H	Z	E	F	U	V	U	T	E	Y
S	G	A	U	T	H	T	O	Q	S
N	W	C	Q	D	B	E	N	S	Y
D	V	D	F	A	V	S	R	T	Q

gl

There are 5 possible words in the puzzle! Have fun!

Write the Words!

Write the words found in the puzzle on the lines below:

Name: _______________________

D	G	E	A	G	R	O	U	P	Z
F	R	M	W	S	H	W	T	I	V
Y	O	G	K	E	Q	K	R	H	P
S	V	R	N	G	R	O	U	T	F
P	E	O	A	G	M	C	F	Y	G
V	M	V	I	R	D	T	C	P	B
U	J	E	D	O	T	K	A	D	F
Z	M	L	X	W	I	T	X	E	X
K	R	U	J	E	Z	U	M	I	P
X	W	M	V	Q	C	B	I	W	Y

Circle the words that contains the consonant blend below:

gr

There are 5 possible words in the puzzle! Have fun!

Write the Words!

Write the words found in the puzzle on the lines below:

P	H	G	P	K	K	K	K	C	H
I	V	S	G	P	P	L	A	I	N
O	P	T	M	U	L	S	P	N	M
I	P	L	O	G	C	A	W	P	Q
B	U	I	A	L	P	K	N	A	I
L	W	U	P	N	L	F	M	E	P
O	S	D	I	V	A	X	F	N	T
X	Z	X	C	Y	N	R	A	D	H
P	L	A	N	E	K	O	V	M	G
O	M	H	V	O	K	B	X	Y	Z

Circle the words that contains the consonant blend below:

pl

There are 5 possible words in the puzzle! Have fun!

Write the Words!

Write the words found in the puzzle on the lines below:

O	P	R	I	Z	E	D	F	I	X
H	M	S	R	R	O	I	I	Q	I
B	E	Y	V	B	I	Z	N	N	N
L	N	L	P	F	I	L	O	Z	I
F	P	E	R	L	S	V	E	R	B
W	Y	P	O	F	L	C	D	D	P
P	R	O	B	L	E	M	W	O	R
G	P	P	E	P	S	V	M	U	I
B	N	J	F	A	J	Z	L	T	N
X	S	G	P	R	O	J	E	C	T

Circle the words that contains the consonant blend below:

dr

There are 5 possible words in the puzzle! Have fun!

Write the Words!

Write the words found in the puzzle on the lines below:

P	I	R	I	K	C	X	F	G	O
C	G	D	Z	Q	Y	R	P	U	S
O	R	B	H	W	W	C	Y	G	K
C	P	U	W	R	X	G	S	I	R
R	V	I	X	E	N	I	L	S	F
Y	K	R	T	U	D	T	F	B	Y
P	V	Y	H	V	C	R	Y	P	T
T	C	T	G	K	X	V	A	N	I
I	H	N	V	H	U	P	K	G	K
C	C	R	Y	S	T	A	L	C	I

Circle the words that contains the consonant blend below:

dr

There are 5 possible words in the puzzle! Have fun!

Write the Words!

Write the words found in the puzzle on the lines below:

GOOD JOB!

Answers

Form words with the consonant blend bl.
Add the end of the word to bl and write it below.
Say the word. For example: bl + imp = blimp

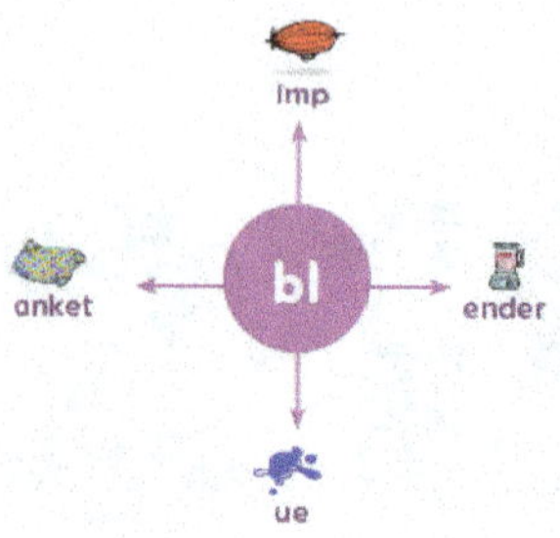

1 blimp
2 blanket
3 blender
4 blue

Form words with the consonant blend br.
Add the end of the word to br and write it below.
Say the word. For example: br + ead = bread

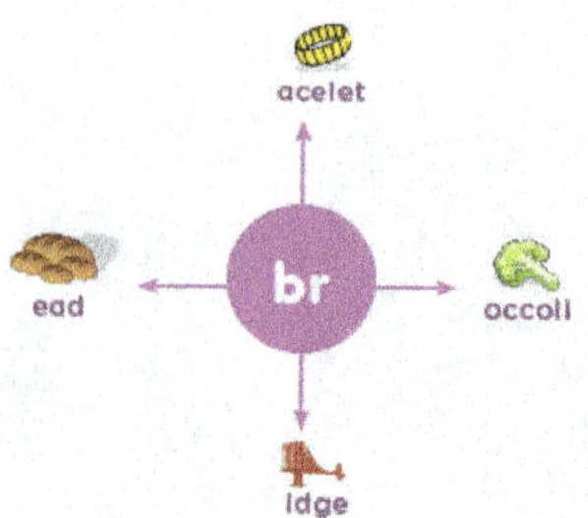

1 bread
2 bracelet
3 broccoli
4 bridge

Form words with the consonant blend cl.
Add the end of the word to cl and write it below.
Say the word. For example: cl + ock = clock

1 clock
2 clown
3 cleaver
4 cloud

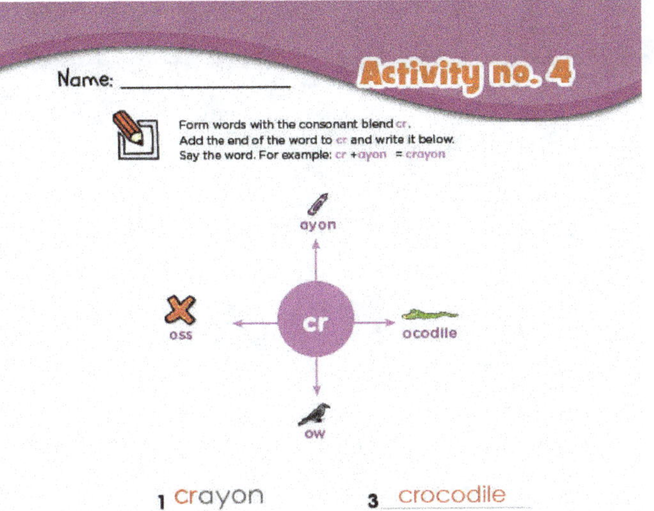

Name: _______________
Activity no. 4

Form words with the consonant blend cr.
Add the end of the word to cr and write it below.
Say the word. For example: cr +ayon = crayon

ayon
oss
cr
ocodile
ow

1 crayon   3 crocodile
2 cross   4 crow

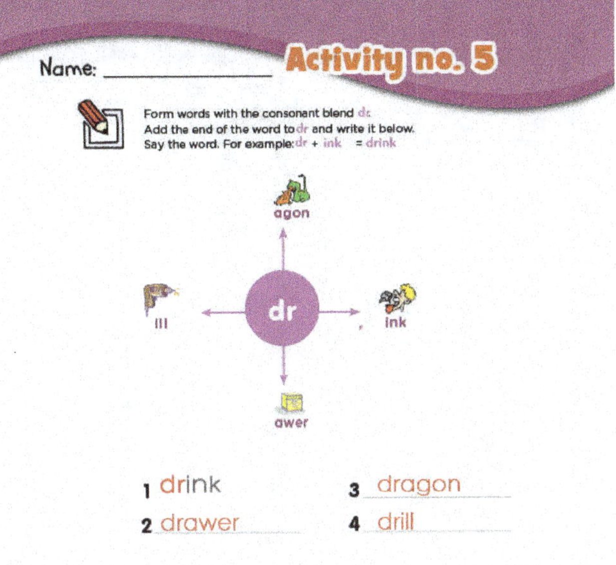

Name: _______________
Activity no. 5

Form words with the consonant blend dr.
Add the end of the word to dr and write it below.
Say the word. For example: dr + ink = drink

agon
ill
dr
ink
awer

1 drink   3 dragon
2 drawer   4 drill

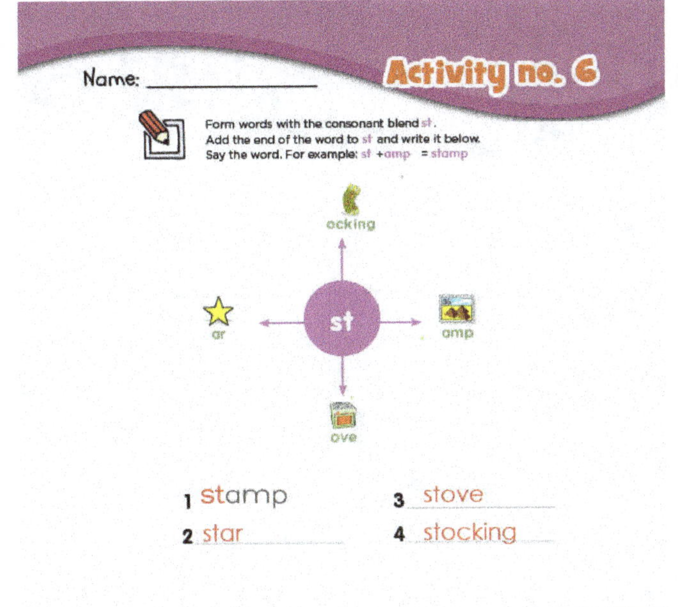

Name: _______________
Activity no. 6

Form words with the consonant blend st.
Add the end of the word to st and write it below.
Say the word. For example: st +amp = stamp

ocking
ar
st
amp
ove

1 stamp   3 stove
2 star   4 stocking

Activity no. 7

Form words with the consonant blend fl .
Add the end of the word to fl and write it below.
Say the word. For example: fl + ower = flower

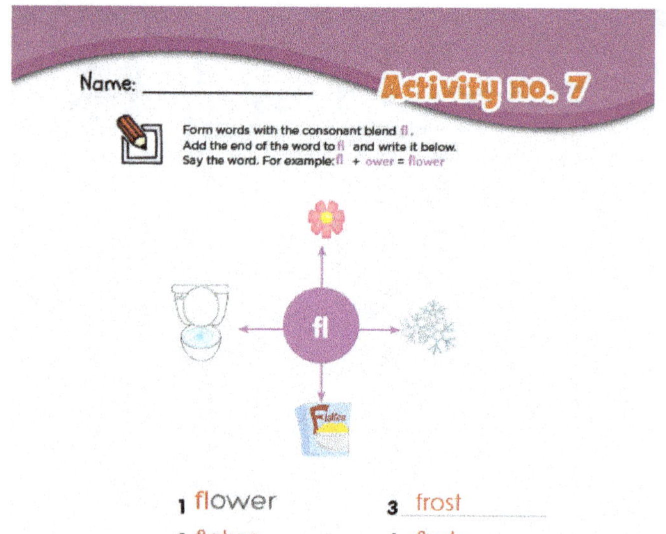

1 flower   3 frost
2 flakes   4 flush

Activity no. 8

Form words with the consonant blend sl .
Add the end of the word to sl and write it below.
Say the word. For example: sl +lice   = sllice

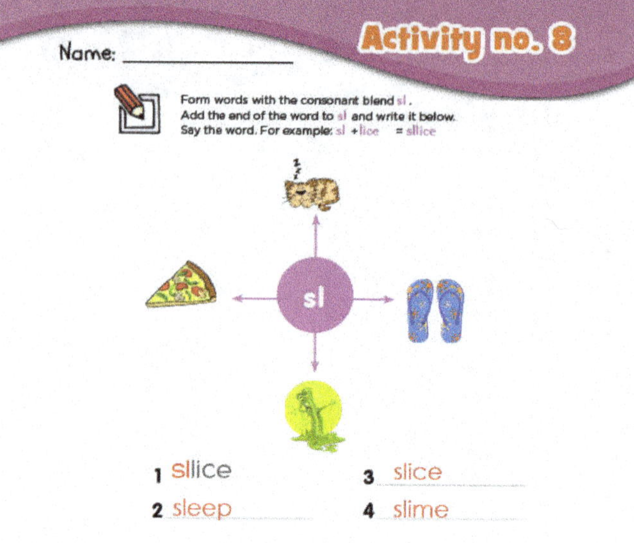

1 sllice   3 slice
2 sleep   4 slime

Activity no. 3

Form words with the consonant blend cl .
Add the end of the word to cl and write it below.
Say the word. For example: cl + ock = clock

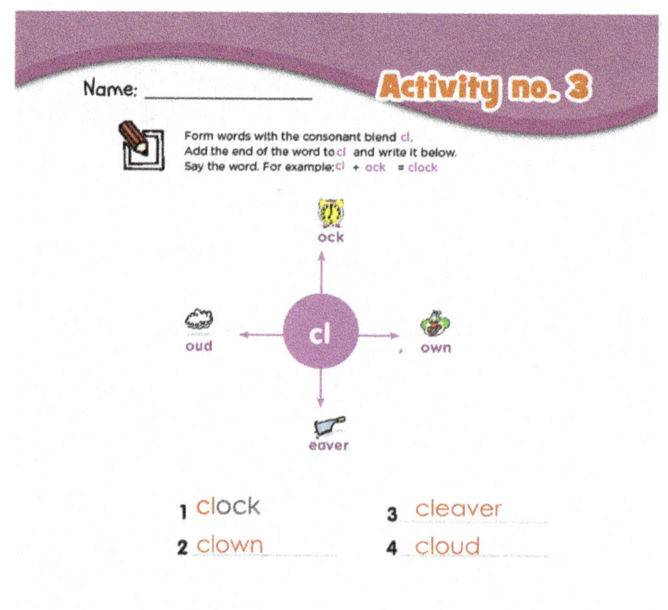

1 clock   3 cleaver
2 clown   4 cloud

Form words with the consonant blend sh.
Add the end of the word to sh and write it below.
Say the word. For example: sh + ip = ship

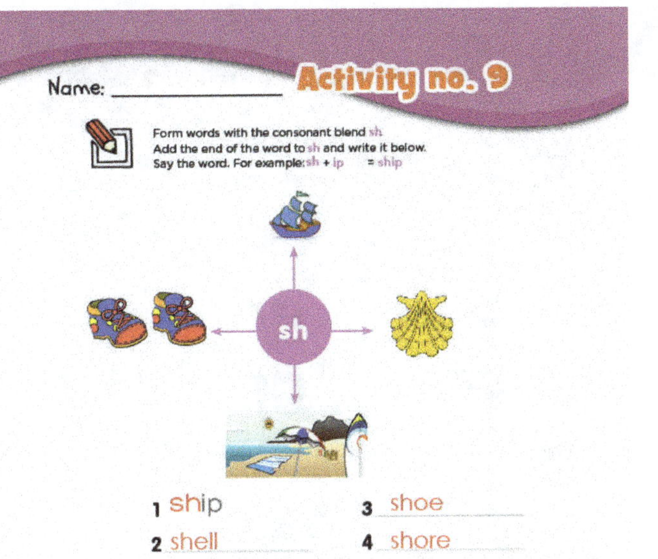

1 ship   3 shoe

2 shell   4 shore

Form words with the consonant blend sk.
Add the end of the word to sk and write it below.
Say the word. For example: sk + y = sky

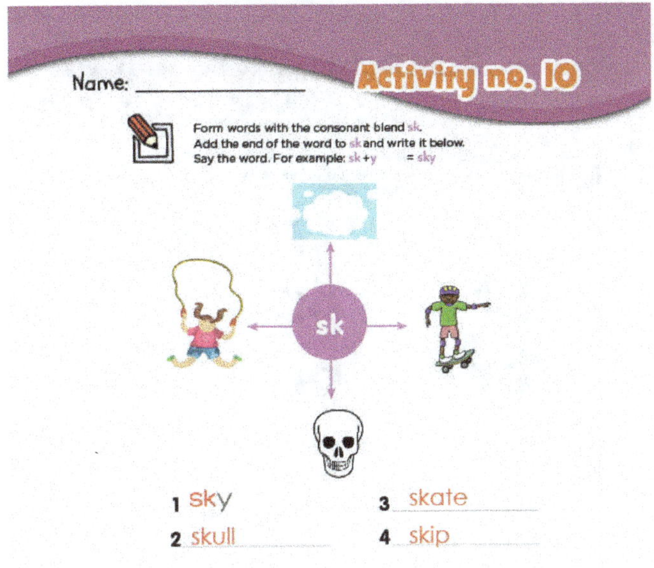

1 sky   3 skate

2 skull   4 skip

Form words with the consonant blend sm.
Add the end of the word to sm and write it below.
Say the word. For example: sm + all = small

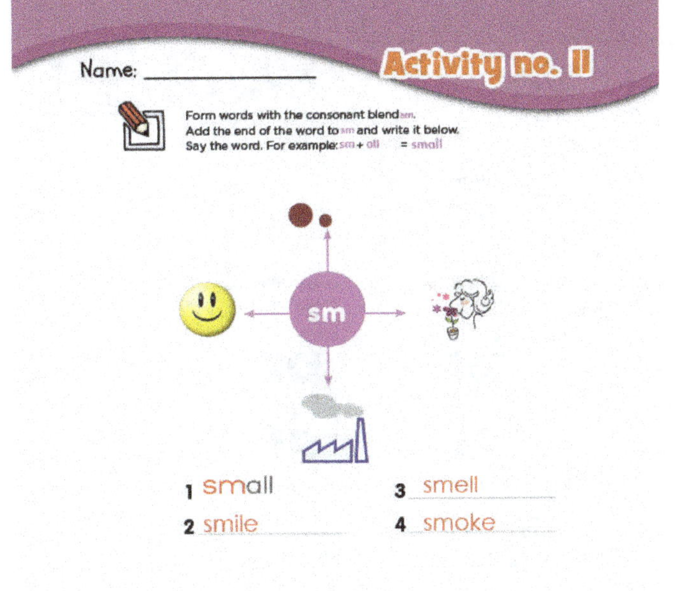

1 small   3 smell

2 smile   4 smoke

First, say the word. Add the correct missing letters to complete the word. Compare the sounds of the words with br against those with pr.

br   **pr**

bride   **pr**ide

bray   **pr**ay

Read the sentences below and underline words with br or pr.

First, say the word. Add the correct missing letters to complete the word. Compare the sounds of the words with cr against those with gr.

cr   **gr**

cross   **gr**oss

crew   **gr**ew

Read the sentences below and underline words with cr or gr.

First, say the word. Add the correct missing letters to complete the word. Compare the sounds of the words with dr against those with tr.

dr   **tr**

brain   **pr**ain

brip   **pr**ip

drunk   **dr**unk

Read the sentences below and underline words with dr or tr.

First, say the word. Add the correct missing letters to complete the word. Compare the sounds of the words with **fr** against those with **fl**.

fr   **fl**

fr___y   **fl**___y

fr___og   **fl**___og

Read the sentences below and underline words with **fr** or **fl**.

Say the word. Write the correct beginning to complete the word.

chair   **ch**op

chick   **ch**ain

Say the sentence. Underline words that start with **ch**.

Say the word. Write the correct beginning to complete the word.

ship   **gr**op

croe   **gr**eep

Say the sentence. Underline words that start with **sh**.

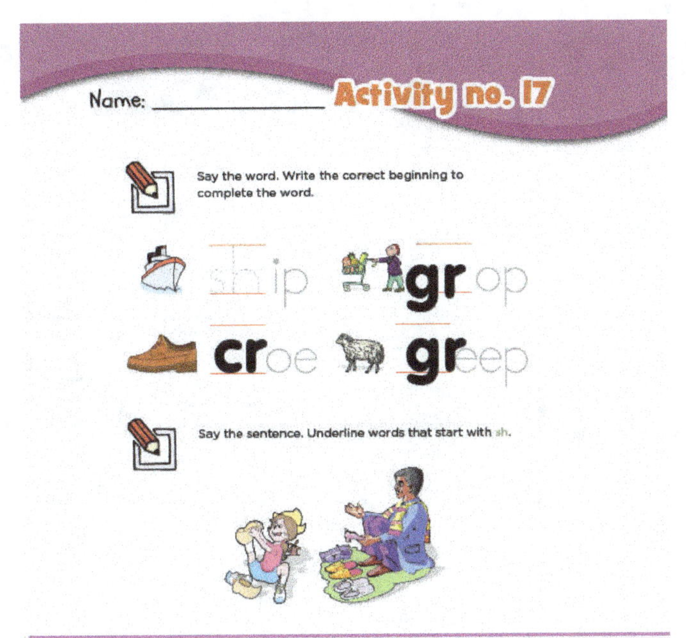

Activity no. 18

Name: _______________

Say the word. Write **th** at the beginning of each word, to complete the words with the voiceless /th/ sound.

3 three   👍 **th**umb

🐵 **dr**ink   🏃 **th**row

Say the sentence below. Underline words that start with **th**.

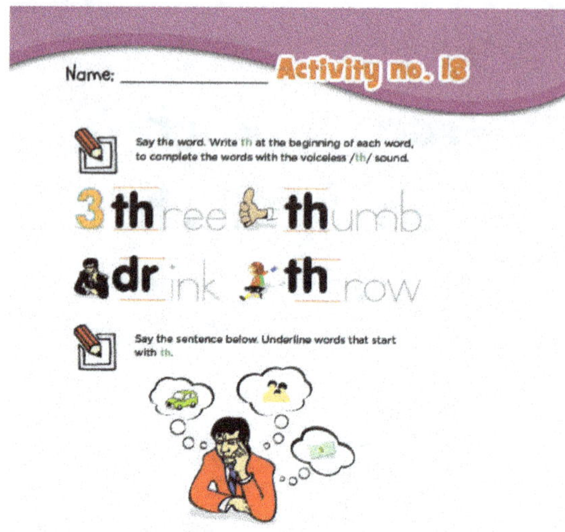

Activity no. 19

Name: _______________

The letters **wh** make the sound /hw/ as in whale. Say the word. Write the correct beginning to complete the word.

🐋   ☸

whale   **wh**eel

Trace the first words of the questions. Read the questions.

What is your name?

When is your birthday?

Why are you late?

Activity no. 20

Name: _______________

The digraph **ph** makes the sound /f/ as in photo. Trace the letters and say the word.

📱 **ph**one   🖼 **ph**oto

🐦 **ph**easant

🧑 **ph**otogra**ph**er

🐘 ele**ph**ant

Read the sentences below. Circle words with **ph** or **f**. Say the words again.

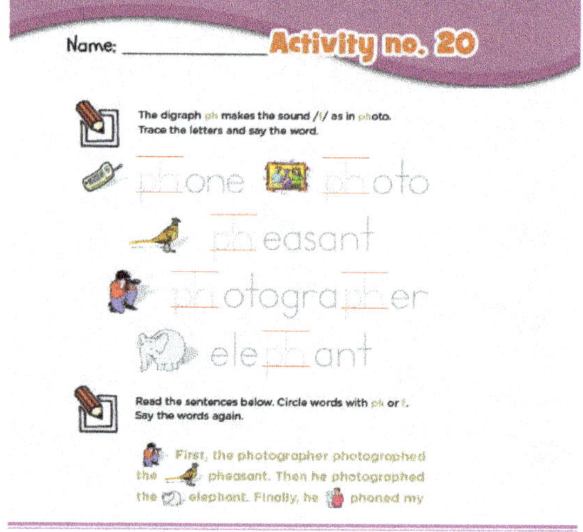

Activity no. 21

Name: _______________

First, say the word. Add the correct missing letters to complete the word. Compare the sounds of the words with **spl** against those with **spr**.

spl   **spr**

splint   **spr**int

splay   **spr**ay

Read the sentences below and underline words with **spl** or **spr**.

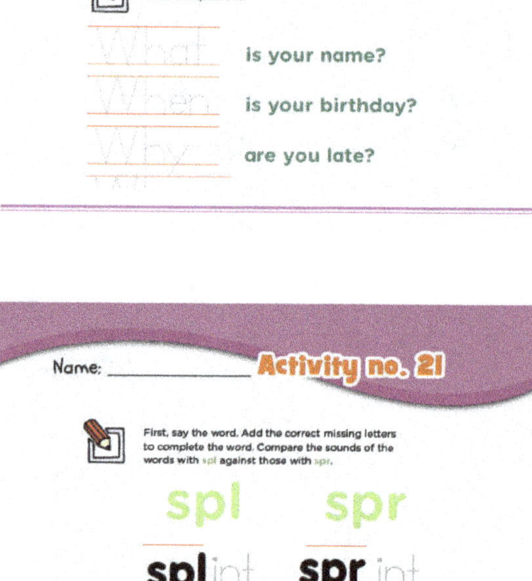

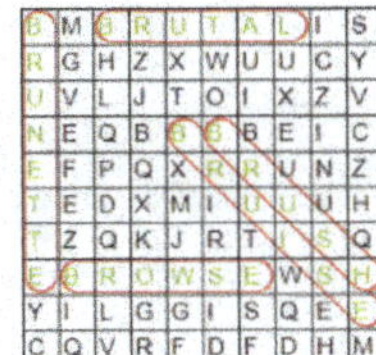

Circle the words that contains the consonant blend below:

br

There are 5 possible are there!

Have fun!

Write the Words!

Write the words found in the puzzle on the lines below:

blurry

blurt

blush

bluster

blustery

Circle the words that contains the consonant blend below:

ch

There are 5 possible are there!

Have fun!

Write the Words!

Write the words found in the puzzle on the lines below:

church

choose

chop

chose

chore

Circle the words that contains the consonant blend below:

cl

There are 5 possible are there!

Have fun!

Write the Words!

Write the words found in the puzzle on the lines below:

clumsy
clunky
cluster
clutch
clutter

Circle the words that contains the consonant blend below:

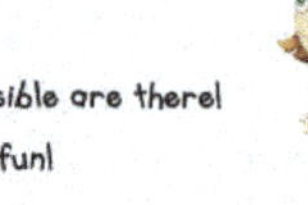

dr

There are 5 possible are there!

Have fun!

Write the Words!

Write the words found in the puzzle on the lines below:

drug
drum
drunk
dry
dry

Circle the words that contains the consonant blend below:

U	F	O	I	S	O	S	S	W
W	I	K	I	L	I	E	S	Y
J	Z	I	M	L	D	T	H	A	R
P	L	I	R	G	S	Q	H	F
I	F	I	I	P	Q	N	G	X	L
F	H	P	O	F	G	M	O	N	O
G	V	Q	A	C	L	O	C	K	E
D	K	Q	U	O	B	P	A	X	N
R	D	D	A	A	F	P	A	E	T
R	R	M	A	D	S	W	F	N	V

fl

There are 5 possible are there!

Have fun!

Write the Words!

Write the words found in the puzzle on the lines below:

flit

float

flock

floe

flog

Circle the words that contains the consonant blend below:

Q	R	K	G	L	U	M	T	R	B
M	K	P	Q	J	L	W	Y	C	N
L	J	V	M	F	V	J	G	U	A
D	F	J	U	M	P	G	L	U	E
R	N	T	C	G	Y	G	U	I	K
N	D	S	P	I	Q	I	T	V	E
H	Z	E	F	U	V	U	T	E	Y
S	G	A	U	T	H	I	O	Q	S
N	W	C	Q	D	B	E	N	S	Y
D	V	D	F	A	V	S	R	T	Q

gl

There are 5 possible are there!

Have fun!

Write the Words!

Write the words found in the puzzle on the lines below:

glue

glum

glut

glutes

glutton

Circle the words that contains the consonant blend below:

gr

There are 5 possible are there!

Have fun!

Write the Words!

Write the words found in the puzzle on the lines below:

group

grout

grove

grovel

grow

Circle the words that contains the consonant blend below:

pl

There are 5 possible are there!

Have fun!

Write the Words!

Write the words found in the puzzle on the lines below:

plain

plan

plane

planet

plank

Circle the words that contains the consonant blend below:

pr

There are 5 possible are there!

Have fun!

Write the Words!

Write the words found in the puzzle on the lines below:

print

prize

probe

problem

project

Circle the words that contains the consonant blend below:

dr

There are 5 possible are there!

Have fun!

Write the Words!

Write the words found in the puzzle on the lines below:

cry

crux

crypt

crystal

cryptic

Visit
BABY PROFESSOR
EDUCATION KIDS
www.BabyProfessorBooks.com
to download Free Baby Professor eBooks and view
our catalog of new and exciting Children's Books

www.ingramcontent.com/pod-product-compliance
Lightning Source LLC
Chambersburg PA
CBHW080254180726
47999CB00018B/2665